LIGHTNING BOLT BOOKS™

Cool Stock Cars

Jon M. Fishman

Lerner Publications ◆ Minneapolis

Lerner Publications Company
A division of Lerner Publishing Group, Inc.
241 First Avenue North
Minneapolis, MN 55401 USA

For reading levels and more information, look up this title at www.lernerbooks.com.

Library of Congress Cataloging-in-Publication Data

The Cataloging-in-Publication Data for *Cool Stock Cars* is on file at the Library of Congress.
ISBN 978-1-5415-1993-0 (lib. bdg.)
ISBN 978-1-5415-2759-1 (pbk.)
ISBN 978-1-5415-2511-5 (eb pdf)

Manufactured in the United States of America
1-44329-34575-11/22/2017

Table of Contents

It's a Stock Car!

Zoom! Three stock cars speed down the racetrack. Their mighty engines roar. The cars cross the finish line. It's a photo finish!

The shape of stock cars is like the shape of regular cars. But stock cars have special parts that make them different from regular cars.

Stock cars have much more powerful engines than regular cars.

People build stock cars for racing. They are made to go fast and keep drivers safe.

NASCAR oversees stock car races in the United States and other countries.

Thousands of fans sit in the stands to watch a NASCAR race.

The Stock Car Story

People have enjoyed race cars ever since they were invented in the late nineteenth century. The first stock car races took place in the United States in the early twentieth century.

The first stock car race was held at Daytona Beach in 1936.

The first NASCAR race was in 1948. NASCAR organized races and set rules for stock cars.

In 1959, NASCAR held the first Daytona 500. The race became popular, and NASCAR grew quickly in the 1960s.

The Daytona 500 is one of the world's most famous auto races.

Companies such as M&M's pay NASCAR teams to advertise on the cars.

Current NASCAR drivers earn points during the season based on how they finish races. The winner of a race gets the most points. Then NASCAR names a champion at the end of the season.

Stock Car Parts

A stock car speeds around a curve in a track. It is going too fast! The car crashes into two others. Pieces fly from the cars as they crash.

Stock cars have light bodies. The bodies cover strong metal frames. The frames protect drivers during crashes.

Drivers are strapped into their seats to keep them safe in case of an accident.

A spoiler rises from the back of a stock car. Air rushes past the spoiler. The air pushes down on the spoiler.

Air flows around this spoiler and pushes the car down to stay on the track.

The term *horsepower* comes from comparing the power of an engine to the power of one horse.

Vroom! Vroom! A NASCAR driver steps on the gas pedal. Stock car engines can make more than 800 horsepower.

Stock Cars in Action

Woo-hoo! Fans cheer and take photos during the Daytona 500. Forty stock cars are racing for millions of dollars in prize money.

A pit stop may take just twelve seconds.

A stock car turns away from the track. It makes a pit stop. **Workers fill the car with gas and change its tires.**

A driver makes her move and whizzes past other racers. Stock cars can go more than 200 miles (322 km) per hour.

Stock cars go more than three times faster than most cars drive on a highway.

Racing so fast can be dangerous. NASCAR is working to make races safer for fans and drivers. That way everyone can enjoy a day at the racetrack!

Stock Car Diagram

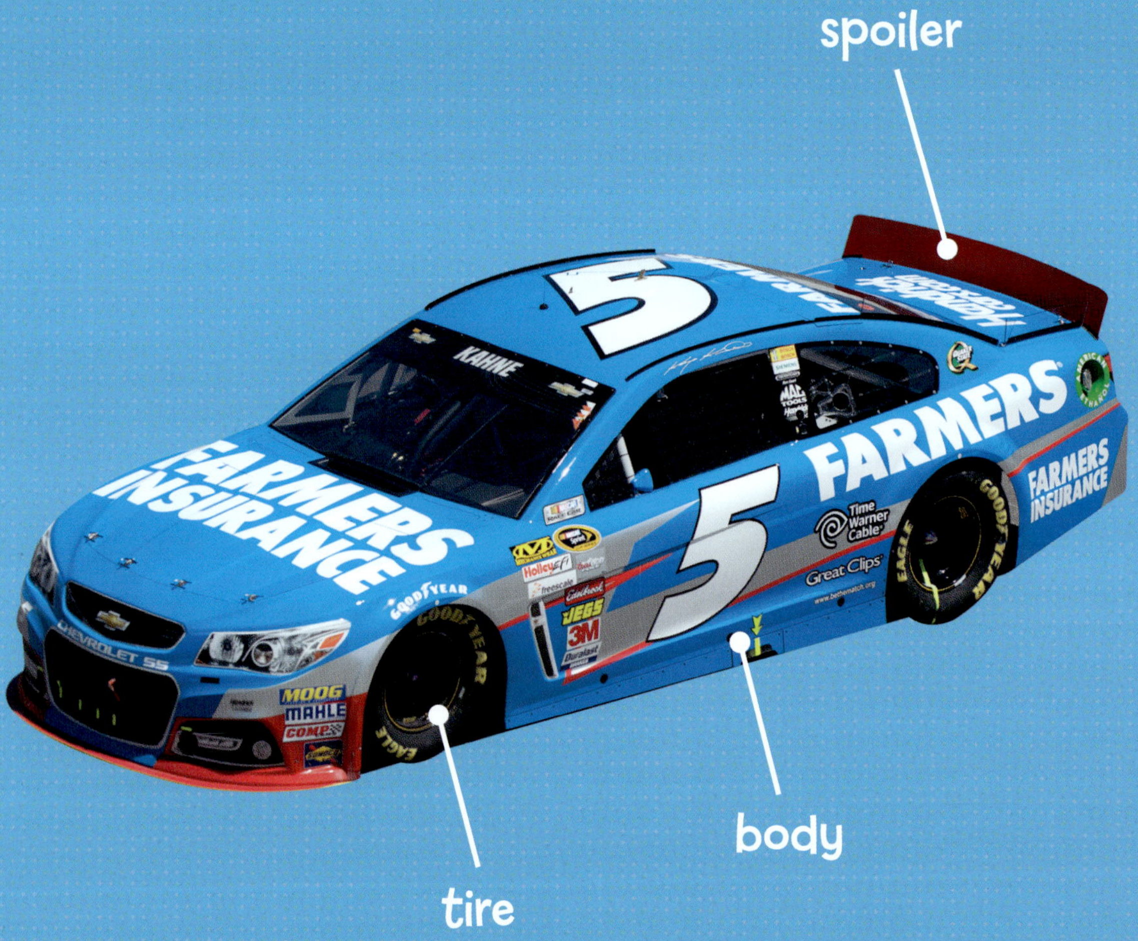

Stock Car Facts

- Racing legend Richard Petty won 200 NASCAR races. No other driver has won more than 105 races.
- NASCAR officials send messages to drivers during races by using colored flags. For example, a yellow flag means there has been a crash on the track.
- One way that NASCAR keeps drivers safe is to make sure they don't drive too fast. Special parts are added to stock cars to slow them down.

Glossary

frame: a structure made of smaller pieces used to support something

gas pedal: a pedal a driver pushes to send gas to a car's engine

horsepower: a unit that measures the power of an engine. The term *horsepower* comes from comparing the power of an engine to the power of one horse.

NASCAR: National Association for Stock Car Auto Racing

photo finish: a race that is so close at the end that a judge must look at a photograph to see who won

pit stop: a stop during a race for more gas and other service

prize money: money given as an award for winning a race or a race series

Further Reading

Car Racing
https://kids.wclibrary.info/learn/curious_kids/index_car_racing.asp

Crane, Cody. *Race Cars*. New York: Children's Press, 2018.

Facts about Cars
http://www.scienceforkidsclub.com/cars.html

Kortemeier, Todd. *Superstars of NASCAR*. Mankato, MN: Amicus High Interest, 2017.

NASCAR Acceleration Nation for Kids
http://www.accelerationnation.com/index.html

Reinke, Beth Bence. *Race Cars on the Go*. Minneapolis: Lerner Publications, 2018.

Index

Photo Acknowledgments

The images in this book are used with the permission of: Daniel Hurlimann/Shutterstock.com, pp. 2, 6, 17, 18, 20, 23; Brian Lawdermilk/Getty Images, p. 4; Matthew Jacques/Shutterstock.com, p. 5; The George F. Landegger Collection of Alabama Photographs in Carol M. Highsmith's America, Library of Congress, Prints and Photographs Division (LC-DIG-highsm-09115), p. 7; RacingOne/Getty Images, pp. 8, 9, 10; Action Sports Photography/Shutterstock.com, pp. 11, 12, 16, 19; Natursports/Shutterstock.com, p. 13; PHOTOMDP/Shutterstock.com, p. 14; Hector Vivas/Jam Media/LatinContent/Getty Images, p. 15.

Cover: Sean Gardner/Getty Images.

Main body text set in Billy Infant regular 28/36. Typeface provided by SparkType.